RELEASING
YOUR
SPIRIT

RELEASING
YOUR
SPIRIT

Jessie Penn-Lewis

Whitaker House

Unless otherwise indicated, all Scripture quotations are taken from the *King James Version* (KJV) of the Bible.

Scripture quotations marked (RV) are taken from the *Revised Version* of the Holy Bible.

RELEASING YOUR SPIRIT

ISBN: 0-88368-424-1
Printed in the United States of America
Copyright © 1997 by Whitaker House

Whitaker House
30 Hunt Valley Circle
New Kensington, PA 15068

1 2 3 4 5 6 7 8 9 10 11 12 / 07 06 05 04 03 02 01 00 99 98 97

Contents

1. Spirit, Soul, and Body.................................... 7

2. The Carnal Christian 27

3. The Soul of Man 41

4. Dividing Soul and Spirit 63

5. Laws of the Spirit-Life.............................. 83

6. The Spiritual Christian 97

One

Spirit, Soul, and Body

Spirit, Soul, and Body

Lack of knowledge and misconceptions about an important spiritual truth are very widespread among Christians today. Either can be the primary reason why many devoted and earnest believers are not reaching full spiritual growth, which is meant to be a natural outcome of their faith and discipleship in Christ.

Part of the difficulty lies in the fact that some spiritual concepts are more difficult to grasp than others and require more careful examination to determine their meaning. This problem is compounded when the English language cannot adequately convey the meaning of a particular word in Scripture from the original biblical language.

This is particularly so with the terms *soul* and *spirit*. The fact that most Christians do not understand the distinction between these

9

words is of critical importance. Many believers are unaware that their lack of knowledge regarding these key spiritual concepts is affecting both their spiritual peace and their usefulness to God.

Let us now examine in more detail how this confusion occurred. G. H. Pember identified the reason as the common use of the phrase "body and soul," which reflects a deficiency in the English language. He said that although we have the nouns *spirit* and *soul*, which are too often treated as synonyms, we have no adjective for *soul*. That is, while the adjective for *spirit* is *spiritual*, we do not have a corresponding word for *soul*. The lack of such an adjective has almost omitted any reference to man's tripartite nature (spirit, soul, and body) in our English language versions of the Bible, where, according to Pember, the Greek word that signifies "pertaining to the soul" is sometimes translated *"natural"* and sometimes *"sensual."* (See 1 Corinthians 2:14; 15:46; James 3:15; Jude 19.)

Of course, scholars know well the distinction between the words in the original Greek: spirit—*pneuma,* soul—*psuchē,* flesh—*sarx.* However, the majority of Christians are unaware of these distinctions. The result is that, in their daily lives, they are often unable to discern between the three realms of life in their personal experience. This inability can vitally affect their spiritual peace.

Learning the differences between these terms is not just an academic exercise. It is a matter of spiritual protection. The Devil, who is a fallen archangel and has superhuman wisdom, knows that human beings are made up of spirit, soul, and body. And right now, as an *"angel of light"* (2 Corinthians 11:14), he is using all the power of the knowledge that he possesses to counterfeit the working of the Holy Spirit. He is creating in the souls of believers such perfect imitations of the pure life of the Spirit of God—who indwells their spirits—that the most earnest Christians are liable to be deceived. It is therefore necessary that what the Scriptures teach regarding the distinction between *soul* and *spirit* should be brought within the range of comprehension of even the youngest believer in Christ and made as clear as possible from the Word of God.

In this book, I am not attempting to meet the needs of those who are able to go directly to the Greek New Testament and read the original text for themselves. My purpose is to assist those who must have additional help, as they earnestly seek the aid of the Spirit of God. I desire to enable them to grasp the truth and to receive spiritual understanding of spiritual facts that are outlined in Scripture and that are necessary for their growth in life and godliness.

In light of this, it is important that you make a conscious decision, in faith, to take the promises of John 14:26, *"The Holy Ghost, whom the Father will send in my name, he shall teach you all things,"* and John 16:13, *"He will guide you into all truth,"* with the confidence that the Spirit of God will faithfully instruct those who are teachable children of God.

This will enable you to grasp the truth of God's Word, for when a believer is taught by the Holy Spirit, he is able to learn, through personal experience, the distinction between *soul* and *spirit* without ever knowing the truth intellectually. The opposite is also true. The scholar may know clearly the differences between these words in the original Greek without knowing from experience all that the words mean. That is, he may know the truth intellectually, but not in spiritual power. If this is the case, he only knows the *"letter"* and not the *"spirit"* of the words (2 Corinthians 3:6).

For example, the believer who has been taught personally *"the dividing asunder of soul and spirit"* (Hebrews 4:12) by the Holy Spirit, before comprehending the distinction with his mind, is better able to understand and *"rightly* [divide] *the word of truth"* (2 Timothy 2:15) than someone who can read Greek but who has not yet been taught this principle by God. Behind the words of the Scriptures there are deep spiritual truths that cannot be understood by the *"natural man"* (1 Corinthians 2:14) and can only be known by revelation.

Therefore, trust the Holy Spirit to lead and guide you as you learn the crucial differences between spirit, soul, and body, and their respective functions.

Matters of the Soul

Before we can adequately comprehend the distinctions between spirit, soul, and body, we need to compensate for the missing adjective for *soul*. G. H. Pember wrote that an attempt has been made to use the Greek word *psychic* for expressing the adjective for *soul* in English. The word, however, has other connotations that do not make it appropriate for general use. Pember translated the word *"sensual"* from James 3:15 as "soulish," and this seems to better express what is needed. Stockmayer

13

also used the word *soulish* to signify things that pertain to the soul, for he said, in reference to 1 Corinthians 2:14, "The Greek text has it, the 'soulman,' or 'soulish-man.' As *spiritual* is the adjective of spirit, so is *soulish* the adjective of soul."

The word *soulish*, therefore, might well be generally accepted by English readers as the missing adjective. This will enable us to speak of soulish or *"natural"* (1 Corinthians 2:14) Christians as well as of *"spiritual"* and *"carnal"* (1 Corinthians 3:1) Christians, so that the distinctions between them are clear. Because of this, I will use the word *soulish* as the adjective for *soul* for the purposes of this book.

Now, regarding the difference between the words *soul* and *spirit*, it is striking that, according to Gall, the distinction is made not only in the English language, but also in every classic language beginning with Hebrew. Yet, in English translations of the New Testament, only two passages bring out the distinction clearly: *"Dividing asunder of soul and spirit"* (Hebrews 4:12), and, *"Sanctify you...spirit and soul and body"* (1 Thessalonians 5:23). These two passages, however, are sufficient even for readers of English language Bibles to see that

14

man is tripartite—made up of spirit, soul, and body—and not bipartite—made up of soul and body only.

The Functions of the Soul

Because the soul lies between the spirit and the body, it has a crucial role. That is why, as an introduction to our topic, I now want to spend some time discussing the nature of the soul. How does the soul differ from the spirit and the body, and what are its functions?

Before we go to the Scriptures to answer these questions, I want to present you with the thoughts of other writers on this subject. Their observations will help us to discover what the writer of Hebrews meant by the *"dividing asunder of soul and spirit"* (Hebrews 4:12), so that we may more clearly understand how *"spirit and soul and body"* can be sanctified and *"preserved blameless unto the coming of our Lord Jesus Christ"* (1 Thessalonians 5:23).

G. H. Pember, in his work, *Earth's Earliest Ages,* quoted Tertullian, one of the church fathers who wrote in the early centuries of the Christian era. Tertullian called the flesh, or physical being, the "body of the soul," and he called the soul the "vessel of the spirit." The soul lies between the spirit and the body, he said, for "direct communication between spirit and flesh is impossible; their intercourse can be carried on only by means of a medium." That medium is the soul.

The "soul was the meeting place, the point of union between body and spirit," wrote Dr. Andrew Murray in *The Spirit of Christ.* "Through the body, man—the *'living soul'* (Genesis 2:7)—stood related to the external world of sense." And through the "spirit he stood related to the spiritual world."

Pember explained the functions of body, soul, and spirit very well when he wrote, again in *Earth's Earliest Ages,* "The body we may term the *sense*-consciousness; the soul the *self*-consciousness; and the spirit the *God*-consciousness." In addition, he wrote that the body "gives us the use of the five senses" and the soul gives us the "intellect which aids us in the present state of existence, and the emotions which proceed from the senses." The spirit, however, is the highest part of man, which comes "directly from God, and by which alone we apprehend and worship Him."

Dr. Andrew Murray concurred with this when he wrote, in *The Spirit of Christ,* that the gifts that the soul was endowed with when man became a *"living soul"* (Genesis 2:7) were those of "consciousness, self-determination, or mind and will." These were to be only the "mold or vessel" into which the life of the Spirit was to be received. In concert with Pember's viewpoint, Dr. Murray also wrote, "The spirit is the seat of our God-consciousness; the soul, of our self-consciousness; the body, of our world-consciousness. In the spirit, God dwells; in the soul, self; in the body, sense."

In addition, Pember wrote about the creation of man and how the tripartite being was formed: "God first molded the senseless frame, and then breathed into it the 'breath of lives' (Genesis 2:7; the original is in the plural)." He stated that this "may refer to the fact that the inbreathing of God produced a twofold life— *sensual* (in the meaning of pertaining to the senses) and *spiritual*." He added in a footnote that perhaps the use of the plural in *"breath of lives"* meant that through "the inbreathing of God became the spirit, and at the same time by its action upon the body, produced the soul."

We see, then, that these writers defined the soul in practical terms as the seat of the personality, consisting of the will and the intellect or mind. It is a personal entity that lies between the spirit, with its openness to the spiritual world, and the body, with its openness to the outer world of nature and sense. Moreover, the soul has the power of choice regarding which world will dominate or control the entire man.

When Adam walked in the Garden of Eden, God dwelt in his spirit and dominated his soul—that is, his intellect, mind, and will. Then, through the vessel of the soul, God shone in and through Adam's *"earthen vessel"* (2 Corinthians 4:7)—his body—making it luminous with His light, immune to cold and heat, and able to perfectly fulfill the purpose for which it had been created.

The Fall of Man

However—and it is tragic that a "however" has to be written—man fell, and the Lord God Himself described what the end result was: *"Every imagination of the thoughts of his heart was only evil continually"* (Genesis 6:5). The Fall apparently began in the intellectual component of the soul, for it is written that Eve saw that the tree was *"to be desired to make one wise"* (Genesis 3:6). The appeal of the Serpent was not made to the *"earthen vessel,"* or the outer man, for the body was then perfectly dominated by the spirit. Rather, it was directed to the intellect and understanding of man, and was based on man's lawful desire to advance in knowledge and power in the unseen realm of another world. *"Ye shall be as gods"* (Genesis 3:5), lied the Serpent. He did not say, "Ye shall be as the beasts" created by God! The temptation was knowledge, the very knowledge that God probably meant to give man in due time. Yet, it was sought outside of God's will and was grasped before its time.

Moreover, Eve fell because she yielded to the very temptation that had caused the fall of the Devil himself, for Satan had said, *"I will be like the most High"* (Isaiah 14:14). The Tempter knew how to attract Eve. He suggested that she could have something higher than she possessed, for she was limited by a body made of dust, but had a soul capable of appreciating knowledge and of growing in the nature of God—through its connection with the highest part of her tripartite nature—and it was to this aspect of her being that the Serpent appealed.

The words of the apostle Paul are therefore very significant in connection with this aspect of the Fall, for he said that the *"preaching of the cross...is the power of God"* (1 Corinthians 1:18) to *"destroy the wisdom of the wise"* (v. 19). Sin entered through the avenue of the intellect, but salvation comes by the Cross that destroys the fallen wisdom. It comes through a genuine acceptance of the message of the Cross, for the preaching of *"Christ crucified"* is *"foolishness"* (v. 23) to the wisdom of men.

God, in the depths of His wisdom, provided salvation in a way that deals with the very cause of the Fall! That is why Paul wrote the following:

> *If any man among you seemeth to be*
> *wise in this world, let him become a fool,*
> *that he may be wise. For the wisdom of*
> *this world is foolishness with God.*
> *(1 Corinthians 3:18–19)*

We do not see the full effect of the Fall until years afterward, when the record of the condition of the human race shows that the road downhill was rapid. The so-called wisdom that gave the knowledge of good and evil in the Garden of Eden arrived at its natural outcome in due course. Man completely sank into his fleshly nature, so that the lower part of man's tripartite nature, which he had in common with the animal creation, obtained the upper hand. It was then that God looked down upon the fallen race and said, *"My spirit shall not always strive with man, for that he also is flesh"* (Genesis 6:3). Therefore, not only has *"death reigned"* (Romans 5:14) over the fallen race of Adam, but every human being born in the likeness of the first Adam is *"of the earth, earthy"* (1 Corinthians 15:47) and is dominated by the flesh instead of the spirit. The soul is a slave of the flesh and the earthly life, instead of being a servant of the spirit.

The Condition of Fallen Man

Therefore, the general condition of unregenerate man is this: his spirit is severed from God, fallen, *"alienated from the life of God"* (Ephesians 4:18), and incapable of fellowship with Him. As it says in Ephesians 2:12, his spirit is *"without Christ...and without God."* Secondly, man's soul—his intellect, mind, will, and self-consciousness—may rule over his body, or his body, in its desires and appetites, may enslave and dominate his soul.

However, while the human spirit is dead (Ephesians 2:1) in relation to God, and is in darkness, it remains as full of activity as the mind or body. In some instances, the spiritual part of the unregenerate man may be so large in its capacity that, even in its dark condition, it dominates both soul and body. If this is the case, a person may be said to be "spiritual," in the sense that he manifests more of his spirit than others who are mainly "soulish" or "fleshly." People like this sometimes seek communication with the supernatural world, apart from the Holy Spirit of God, and are often mediums, capable of exercising occult powers such as clairvoyance, which are bestowed upon them by satanic means. Unless the spirit of a person is regenerated and indwelt by the Holy Spirit of God, it is in harmony with the fallen spirits of Satan and is governed by the *"prince of the power of the air, the spirit that now worketh in the children of disobedience"* (Ephesians 2:2).

Therefore, we see that the spirit of man—which was left without God at the Fall—sank down, so to speak, into the vessel of the soul, and the soul, in turn, sank down into the fleshly body, controlled by what the apostle Paul described as the *"desires of the flesh"* (Ephesians 2:3). Pember said that, in the unconverted,

> ...the soul, manifested sometimes in intellectuality, sometimes in sensuality, often in both, reigns over them with undisputed sway. This is what Jude

wishes to set forth in his nineteenth verse, which should be rendered, *"These be they who separate themselves,* [governed by soul], *having not the Spirit."*

Fausset very clearly brought this out in his commentary on Jude 19, for he wrote,

> In the threefold division of man's being...the due state in God's design is that the spirit...should be first, and should rule the soul, which stands intermediate between body and spirit, but in the...natural man, the spirit is sunk into subserviency to the animal-soul, which is earthly in its motives and aims. The carnal sink somewhat lower, for in these the flesh, the lowest element...reigns paramount.

The Cross Is the Remedy

In regeneration, it is the darkened and fallen "spirit of man which is quickened again and renewed," Andrew Murray wrote in his notes to *The Spirit of Christ.* This is the meaning of the Lord's words to Nicodemus. Jesus told this *"master of Israel"* (John 3:19), in spite of all the intellectual religious knowledge that Nicodemus had: *"Ye must be born anew* [or, from above, RV, mg]*"* (v. 7 RV). And later on, He said to His disciples, *"It is the spirit that quickeneth; the flesh profiteth nothing"* (John 6:63).

The way that the new life from above reaches the fallen spirit of man is revealed in these words of our Lord:

> [The Spirit breatheth, RV, mg] *where it listeth, and thou hearest the voice thereof, but knowest not whence it cometh, and whither it goeth: so is every one that is born of the Spirit.*
>
> *(John 3:8 RV)*

The reason the Spirit of God quickens a believer's spirit into new life is given in John 3:14–16. The God-man died on the cross in the place of the sinner, so *"that whosoever believeth* [into, literal Greek] *him should not perish, but have everlasting life"* (v. 16).

The Cross and the Fall exactly and perfectly correspond to each another—the first is the remedy for the second. By the death of the Savior on the cross, sin was *"put away"* (Hebrews 9:26), and the way was made possible for the Holy God to pardon the sinner.

Then, the sinner was given a way of escape from the bondage of soul and body into which he had fallen. It became possible for the tripartite nature of man to be in harmony once more, with the spirit in full control, and the body acting merely as the outward and material vessel—the instrument of the spirit through the soul.

This way of escape from bondage is revealed in many parts of Scripture, where we are taught that the believer is to consider himself *"crucified with Christ"* (Galatians 2:20) and *"dead to sin"* (Romans 6:2). In the next chapter, we will see how this way of escape provides for our deliverance, as we consider the full meaning of the Cross.

Two

The Carnal Christian

The Carnal Christian

*And I, brethren, could not speak unto you as
unto spiritual, but as unto carnal, even as
unto babes in Christ.*
—*1 Corinthians 3:1*

Let me repeat at this point that the soul is
the seat of the self-consciousness—the
personality, the will, and the intellect. It
lies between the spirit, the seat of the God-
consciousness, and the body, the seat of the
sense- or world-consciousness. In Latin, the
word for soul is *anima*—it is the animating
principle of the body. Gall said that the soul
derives its life, or animating power, from either the spirit (the higher part) or the animal
(the lower part).

In this chapter, we will explore the role of
the lower part of our tripartite nature—the
flesh. Although my main focus in this book is

the distinction between spirit and soul, it is essential that believers first understand how to be set free from being dominated by the flesh so that they can live in the realm of the spirit, which was created to govern both soul and body.

Three Types of Christians

There are only two classes of men: saved and unsaved, unregenerate and regenerate. A person who has been converted has had his spirit regenerated or quickened into life. New life has been communicated to his fallen spirit by the Spirit of God. As Gall indicated, the believer's soul, however, may be dominated either from beneath, by the "animal life," or from above, by the "spirit life." Therefore, there are different classes of believers, described according to their knowledge of God's Word and their growth in the life of Christ. In light of this truth, the Scriptures clearly refer to three types of Christians:

1. The spiritual Christian—dominated by the Spirit of God, who indwells and energizes his renewed human spirit.

2. The soulish Christian—dominated by his soul, that is, his intellect or emotions.

3. The carnal Christian—dominated by his flesh or by fleshly habits: the power or *"the desires of the flesh"* (Ephesians 2:3).

Let us look more closely at what it means to be a carnal Christian.

Walking according to the Flesh

The Greek word in 1 Corinthians 3:1 that is contrasted with *"spiritual"* is not *soul (psuchē)* but *"carnal" (sarkikos)*. This is also the adjective of the word that is used in Romans 8:7, where it is written that *"the carnal* [sarx] *mind is enmity against God."* The Scriptures do not say that the *psuchē,* or soulish, life is enmity against God, but that the *sarkikos,* or fleshly, mind is. It is true that the *"natural"* (soulish, *psuchikos*) man cannot understand the things of the Spirit, as we read in 1 Corinthians 2:14. However, he is not in enmity simply because he is soulish.

According to Fausset, the apostle Paul was saying to the Corinthians, in effect:

And I [as the natural man—"man of soul," Greek—cannot receive, so I, also] *could not speak unto you the deep things of God, as I would to the spiritual; but I was compelled to speak to you as I would to men of flesh.*
(1 Corinthians 3:1, Fausset's paraphrase)

Although the Corinthians were truly regenerate and belonged to Christ, they were dominated by the flesh to such an extent that Paul could only describe them as still *"carnal,"* or fleshly. This was proven by the fact that the works of the flesh were clearly evident among them in *"envying"* and *"strife"* (1 Corinthians 3:3). As Paul wrote to the Galatians:

Now the works of the flesh are manifest, which are these; adultery, fornication, uncleanness, lasciviousness, idolatry, witchcraft, hatred, variance, emulations, wrath, strife, seditions, heresies, envyings, murders, drunkenness, revellings, and such like. *(Galatians 5:19–21)*

Any of these manifestations in a believer reveals the activity, to some degree, of the *sarkikos,* or fleshly, life, which is being exposed through the avenue of the soul. A person who demonstrates these traits is not a soulish person but is a person who is walking *"after the flesh"* (Romans 8:1), even though his spirit may have been renewed by the Spirit of God. The Scripture says that those who are *"in the flesh cannot please God"* (v. 8).

The apostle's description of these Corinthian believers as being *"carnal"* and yet *"babes in Christ"* clearly shows that those who are new in Christ are generally under the domination of the flesh at the initial stage of their spiritual lives. According to Romans 8:8, they are *"in the flesh."* By their regeneration, they are truly in Christ. They have been vitally made alive with Christ's life and planted into Him by His Spirit. As it is written in John 3:16, *"Whosoever believeth* [into, literal Greek] *him should not perish, but have everlasting life."* However, these babes in Christ, who are alive in Him by a living faith, have not yet comprehended all that the Cross severed them from when they were baptized into His death (Romans 6:3) and made alive by His life (v. 11).

From the apostle's statement, it appears that he blames these Corinthians for still being *"babes,"* for the baby stage should not last very long (Hebrews 5:11–14). The regeneration of a person's spirit comes through the inbreathing of life from the Spirit of God, as a result of a person's simple faith in the atoning sacrifice of the Son of God on the cross on his behalf. Yet, this regeneration should be quickly followed by a personal understanding of what it means to be *"crucified with Christ"* (Galatians 2:20) and *"dead to sin"* (Romans 6:2). This brings about deliverance from living a life according to the flesh, a deliverance that the Corinthian Christians had obviously not yet known. The apostle very clearly outlined the characteristics of the carnal Christian. Every believer today, using these traits as a guide, can judge for himself whether he, too, is *"yet carnal"* (1 Corinthians 3:3).

The Deliverance of the Cross

"They that are Christ's have crucified the flesh" (Galatians 5:24). These are the words with which the apostle ended his vivid description of the *"works of the flesh"* (v. 19) in his letter to the Galatians, contrasting them with the *"fruit of the Spirit"* (v. 22) that the Christian should exhibit in his life as he allows the Holy Spirit to rule his spirit.

Babes in Christ who are still carnal need a fuller understanding of the meaning of the Cross, for in the purpose of God the death of Christ means that our *"old man"* (Romans 6:6) was crucified with Him, so that *"they that are Christ's have crucified the flesh with the affections and lusts"* (Galatians 5:24). These refer to strong desires, whether of jealousy or passion.

The same Cross that was revealed to the unregenerate man as the place where his sin was atoned for, and where his burden of sin was removed by the blood of the Lamb, is the place where the carnal Christian must obtain deliverance from the domination of the flesh. A person may be a babe in Christ even though he may have been regenerate for many years. If this is the case, he must obtain deliverance so that he may walk according to the spirit and *"not after the flesh"* (Romans 8:4). In this way, he will become spiritual in due time, a full-grown man in Christ.

The Magna Carta of Spiritual Liberty

The sixth chapter of Romans is the Magna Carta of spiritual liberty because it reveals God's plan of deliverance through the Cross of

Christ. Every babe in Christ needs to know the truth of this passage of Scripture. Romans 6 very clearly explains the basis of deliverance, while there is only a brief reference to it in Galatians 5:24 and other passages.

Only by understanding what it means to have died with Christ (Romans 6:3–8), and what it means to put to death the *"deeds of the body"* (Romans 8:13), can the believer live and walk and act through the Spirit, and in this way become a spiritual man. Paul wrote to the Romans,

> *When we were in the flesh, the motions of sins, which were by the law, did work in our members to bring forth fruit unto death. But now we are delivered from the law, that being dead wherein we were held; that we should serve in newness of spirit, and not in the oldness of the letter.* (Romans 7:5–6)

"In the likeness of sinful flesh" (Romans 8:3), the pure and holy Son of God hung upon the tree, an offering for sin. Because He died for sin and died to sin in the place of the sinner, God has condemned forever a life of *"sin in the flesh"* (Romans 8:3) in all who are truly

united to His Son. It is true that the believer lives *"in the flesh"* (2 Corinthians 10:3), in the sense that he is still in his physical body. However, once he fully comprehends that God's own Son hung upon the tree in the likeness of sinful flesh, and once he knows that he died to sin through Christ's sacrifice, from that point on he lives in the flesh as far as his physical body is concerned, but he does not walk any longer according to the flesh. In other words, he no longer lives according to the demands and desires of his body, but he lives according to the Spirit (Romans 8:5), according to his renewed spirit that is indwelt by the Spirit of God (v. 9).

Based upon the work of the Son of God on the cross of Calvary, in which the sinner was identified with the Substitute who died for him, the redeemed and regenerate believer is called to *"reckon"* or consider himself *"dead indeed unto sin"* (Romans 6:11) because *"our old man is crucified with* [Christ]*"* (v. 6). The Holy Spirit of God who dwells in his spirit can then carry out the divine purpose to its ultimate degree. The *"body of sin"* (v. 6)—that is, the entire mass of sin that dwells throughout the fallen man—may be *"destroyed"* (v. 6) as the believer, on his part, steadily and faithfully refuses to let sin reign (Romans 6:6, 11–14) in his life. The root word *katargeo*, which has been translated in Romans 6:6 as *"destroyed,"* means "to abolish, to leave unemployed, to make barren, to do away with, to render useless." Whatever its best translation, it is clear that the *"body of sin"* is to cease to have any power to cause the believer to be *"entangled again with the yoke of bondage"* (Galatians 5:1) of sin.

As the babe in Christ comes to know and to practice this, his flesh ceases to have control over him, and he rises into real union with the ascended Lord. He is *"alive unto God through Christ Jesus"* (Romans 6:11). The babe in Christ who comprehends this knows the fuller meaning of being alive to God. As he walks according to his spirit, which is yielding to the control and direction of the Spirit of God, he ceases to fulfill the desires of the flesh. He gives his spirit, which is indwelt by the Spirit of God, domination over his entire being. This does not mean that he might not again lapse into walking according to the flesh. However, as long as he sets his mind on *"the things of the Spirit"* (Romans 8:5) and considers himself continually *"dead indeed unto sin"* (Romans 6:11), he *"through the Spirit* [will] *mortify the deeds of the body"* (Romans 8:13) and walk *"in newness of life"* (Romans 6:4).

Ultimately, the complete abolishment of the *"body of sin"* (v. 6)—which includes all that we received in our natures from the first Adam—will be totally accomplished when we are *"fashioned like unto his glorious body"* (Philippians 3:21) at the coming of the Lord from heaven.

Three

The Soul of Man

The Soul of Man

*But the natural man receiveth not the things of
the Spirit of God: for they are foolishness unto
him: neither can he know them, because they
are spiritually discerned.*
—1 Corinthians 2:14

C hristians who have arrived at the stage
where they understand the way of the
cross, where they have ceased to walk
according to the flesh, think that they are now
"spiritual" believers who are entirely renewed
and led by the Spirit of God. However, Andrew
Murray wrote in *The Spirit of Christ* that at
this stage Christians face their most important
lesson regarding the spiritual life. He wrote of
the danger of the "inordinate activity of the
soul, with its power of mind and will," the
"greatest danger [that] the church, or individual, has to dread." Let us examine this danger
more closely.

The believer who has been regenerated in his spirit is *"born of the Spirit"* (John 3:6). The Spirit of God now dwells in his spirit. He has had the revelation of the Cross that has shown him how to overcome living a life according to the flesh. He now walks *"in newness of life"* (Romans 6:4) and in victory over sin (1 Corinthians 15:56–57)—over the sins that are manifested in the *"works of the flesh"* (Galatians 5:19–21).

But, at this stage, certain questions must be asked: What about the soul—the person himself in his personality and in his intellectual and emotional faculties? Which power is animating his actions apart from the works of the flesh? Is he animated and governed in the ordinary activities of his mind, sensibilities, and all the functions included in the word *soul,* by the *"life-giving spirit"* (1 Corinthians 15:45 RV) who comes from above—from the risen Lord as the Second Adam—or from the life that comes from the lower realm, the fallen life of the first Adam?

The prevailing idea in the church is that when the believer has come to understand that he is *"crucified with Christ"* (Galatians 2:20) and *"dead to sin"* (Romans 6:2), and when he ceases to walk habitually *"after the flesh"*

(Romans 8:1), he becomes spiritual and is entirely sanctified from sin and unrighteousness. However, to be delivered from the domination of the flesh, or the carnal life, does not mean that a person ceases to be soulish. Death to sin and the crucifixion of the flesh involve only one stage of the work of the Spirit of God that needs to be accomplished in redeemed man. A believer may cease to be ruled by the flesh (*sarx*) and still be ruled by the soul (*psuchē*). In other words, he may be living in the realm of the soul instead of the spirit, which is the God-conscious sphere.

Characteristics of the Soulish Christian

To understand this clearly, we must learn what it means for a Christian to be soulish, even after he ceases "*to be carnally minded*" (Romans 8:6) or to live "*after the flesh*" (v. 13).

The soul, as we have seen, includes the intellect and the emotions as well as the central personality that makes it the seat of the self-consciousness. A believer may be entirely freed from the obvious works of the flesh that are described in Galatians 5:19–21, while his intellect and emotions are still controlled by the soulish life. In other words, his soul has not yet been fully renewed and animated by God so that the Holy Spirit may work through his regenerated human spirit without any hindrance. The soulish Christian is therefore one whose intellect and emotions are still governed by the life of the first Adam, and not by the life of the Second Adam. The Second Adam sent us the *"life-giving spirit"* (1 Corinthians 15:45 RV), who brings the intellect and emotions under full control as the believer walks according to his spirit. In the believer who is soulish, the Holy Spirit dwells in the spirit and enables the person to *"mortify the deeds of the body"* (Romans 8:13), but the believer's intellect and emotions remain governed by the soul.

Soulish Wisdom

If we consider, for instance, the intellectual life, a passage in the epistle of James very clearly shows the distinction between heavenly and soulish wisdom. The apostle wrote that the wisdom that is *"not from above"* is *"earthly, sensual* [soulish], *devilish"* (James 3:15). It produces jealousy and factions, divisions and partisanship. However, *"the wisdom that is from above"* (v. 17), that is from the Spirit of God, is characterized by purity, peaceableness,

46

gentleness, mercy, and good fruits, and is so full of the divine character that it is *"without partiality"* (v. 17). In short, pure heavenly wisdom contains no element of the soulish life—the place of self-consciousness, self-opinions, and self-interest—and therefore causes peace instead of strife and envy. Later on in this chapter, I will discuss how soulish wisdom can be *"devilish"* or *"demoniacal"* (v. 15 RV, mg).

In light of this passage in James, we can clearly understand the condition of the church of God and why it has frequently split up into factions and sects. It is tragic that the works of the flesh in jealousy and dissension cause *"variance* [quarreling]*," "emulations* [conflict]*,"* and *"strife"* (Galatians 5:20) in churches that profess to know and serve God. However, another cause of disunity and separation in the church is the soulish intellect. Pember remarked that the "intellect is not merely fallible, but the most dangerous of all gifts, unless it be guided by the Spirit of God."

Christians often rely upon the intellect in order to grasp divine truths and to understand spiritual principles, yet the Scriptures declare that the soulish man—and this includes even the believer who is still soulish—cannot receive the things of the Spirit, because they can only be discerned spiritually (1 Corinthians 2:14). Therefore, we see professing believers with soulish wisdom handling divine truths in a way that facilitates the work of demons in promoting division among the followers of Christ.

Also, it is the soulish element, manifested in teachers in the church and those who profess to be holy, that is often the cause of separation and disunity. It is true that some people have love in their hearts for those who differ from them. Nevertheless, the differences divide because demonic powers, which are able to work on the soulish element in believers, always emphasize or exaggerate the differences in people's views of truth, instead of the points in which they are in agreement. These demonic powers even drive eager believers to fight for their views of truth in the name of witnessing for God. Sadly, under the pretext of seeking the blessing of others, these believers often unknowingly imitate the Pharisees by traveling *"sea and land to make one proselyte"* (Matthew 23:15).

It is also the soulish element in Christians that insists that others conform to their views of truth to the most minute detail; they *"pay tithe of mint and anise and cummin* [in words, but] *have omitted the weightier matters of the law"* (Matthew 23:23). What they omit is the law of Christ, which requires love and the unity of the Spirit between believers to be the conditions of their growth into *"the unity of the faith"* (Ephesians 4:13).

In brief, the manipulation of the life of the soul by evil supernatural powers is the main cause of divisions and separations among professing Christians, and even among true children of God. As the Scripture says, *"These be they who separate themselves, sensual"* (Jude 19). In this context, *"sensual"* refers to the life of the soul (the "soul-life") rather than to the life of the flesh. Recall that Pember translated *"sensual"* in this verse as "governed by soul." Fausset, in his commentary, translated it literally as "animal-souled."

The way in which the ungoverned life of the soul causes division is brought out in the Revised Version of the Bible, which translates *"separate themselves"* in Jude 19 as *"make separations"*: *"These are they who make separations."* Fausset wrote in his commentary, "Arrogant setting up of themselves, as having greater sanctity; and a wisdom and peculiar doctrine, distinct from others, is implied."

Separating oneself and considering oneself to have greater sanctity than others are always

49

indications of the soulish life. Jesus taught that the world would separate believers; believers should not separate themselves from one another. The Lord said, *"Blessed are ye, when men shall hate you, and when they shall separate you...for the Son of man's sake"* (Luke 6:22). Also, in the seventh chapter of 1 Corinthians, the apostle Paul, when answering a question about separation, wrote, *"Let every man abide in the same calling wherein he was called"* (1 Corinthians 7:20) and *"therein abide with God"* (v. 24).

God Himself will separate those who walk in light and those who live in darkness, through the light of His own presence. Often the one who chooses to walk in darkness will either drive out the one who lives in the light, or will himself be brought into the light. Men can be governed by their souls even when they have the Spirit, and these soulish ones always *"separate themselves"* (Jude 19) and *"make separations"* (v. 19 RV), proving that in some degree—possibly a very small degree—they are soulish and not spiritual.

Soulish Emotions

The other aspect of the soul-life is the emotional component, which proceeds from the bodily senses. This is another way in which a Christian may be swayed by what is soulish and think that it is completely spiritual. Pember wrote that a "knowledge of biblical psychology dissipates the idea that any holy spiritual influence can be set in motion by appeals to the senses." Yet, reaching the spirit through the senses is the purpose of many church services and even evangelistic meetings where the Gospel is proclaimed.

Pember's words on this subject are illuminating. He wrote,

> Splendid buildings, gorgeous vestments, and picturesque rites for the eye, with sweet odors for the scent, and ravishing music for the ear, although they may bewitch one's consciousness with the most agreeable sensation, can penetrate only as far as the soul...[yet] our spirit...does not receive its impressions from the senses, but only from spirit.

Pember also stated that, from God's point of view, the order of the tripartite nature of man is spirit, soul, and body, because "God's influence commences in the spirit, then lays hold of the emotions and the intellect, and lastly begins to curb the body." From the standpoint of Satan, the order is reversed: it is first earthly, then soulish, and finally devilish (James 3:15), because Satan's influence enters by the body, then attacks the soul, and, if possible, gains entry to the spirit.

These are extremely solemn facts. They reveal very clearly why the churches are filled with nominal worshippers of Christ who show no signs that they have the true life of Christ within them! How sad it is that the very presence of these worshippers in the churches shows that within their spirits they are unconsciously yearning for God. In thousands of cases this longing is never satisfied, for only the soul-life is engaged. They are either responding with the intellect to an intellectual presentation of the letter of the truth, or their senses are being gratified by soothing music and the calming influences of an hour of quiet. However, they are not being led into a real worship of God *"in spirit and in truth"* (John 4:23), which alone is acceptable to Him.

Are we to reject all these soulish influences? God forbid. But they will not save a person. They may and do prepare the way by bringing the person within reach of the truth that is presented in the Scriptures, and all these outer things that point us to righteousness have their value and place.

But—and this is the serious danger—influences that penetrate only to the soul and do not reach the spirit in regenerating power are deceptive. They give a person a *"form of godliness* [without the] *power"* (2 Timothy 3:5). They bring faith in Jesus Christ down to the level of heathen philosophies and cults. Therefore, religious men who are merely "men of soul" place the Son of God on an equal status with Muhammad and Confucius, and they discuss Christianity as just one of the religions of the world. Instead, people should be compelled to see, as in the days of the early church at Pentecost, the omnipotent power of God bearing witness to His Son as the only Savior for a lost world.

Moreover, in missions outreaches, the appeal to the senses and emotions of the soul accounts for the large percentage of converts who do not remain in the faith, as well as the short-lived influence of much evangelistic work. In many instances, this is also the reason for the excessive exhaustion of Christian workers and their resulting emotional or physical breakdowns.

A missionary worker recently wrote:

Is it not the exercise of the soulish, or natural man—the glow, feeling, emotion, and energy, in speaking to others publicly or privately—that causes nerve exhaustion? And is it not possible for the Spirit to quicken the truth without the strain or wear and tear of the body? Is it not possible to tell out God's truth with no "excitement," and for God to breathe out His power on others in the words you speak, not through you so much as through your testimony, after it leaves your lips and enters into the minds of others? It does seem as if more work could be done, and with far less fatigue, if my surmise be true.

A person may naturally have a "fiery" disposition; he may sway and move the emotions of others so that they make a profession of faith. However, when this happens, their faith then stands on the influence or wisdom of the person they have listened to and not on the power of God. We can now see what Andrew Murray meant when he wrote that the greatest danger that the church or individual has to dread is the "inordinate activity of the soul, with its power of mind and will." The old

Quakers used to call this tendency "creaturely activity." It is obviously the energy of man being used in the service of God, rather than man seeking in his spirit to cooperate with the Holy Spirit, who has been given to him as the Gift of the risen Son of God.

Because of this, we find the overly intellectual person, who is under the influence of his soul rather than his spirit, dealing with the eternal destinies of immortal souls, and we find the strong-willed person exercising his will and dominant personality over the consciences and lives of others! Therefore, strategies to reach people and bring them to God through events like musical attractions or lectures on popular subjects are only the manifestation of the soul-life in those who desire to help others. Those who are dominated by their souls may be regenerated, but at the same time they do not know the Spirit of God as a Person who dwells in their spirits, who energizes them by His indwelling power and uses them as messengers of God in the salvation of men.

But there is another segment of the Christian church—a much smaller company of people—who, because they know the Spirit of God who dwells within them, are soulish to a much lesser degree. They have a mixture of soul and spirit in their religious experiences. They are not satisfied unless they *feel* the presence of God continually with them in the realm of their self-consciousness. Consequently, although the Holy Spirit dwells in them, they often fall into the realm of the soul-life because they do not understand the spirit-life and how the human spirit is to cooperate with God.

Soulish Affections

The soul does not only consist of the intellect and the emotions; from the Scriptures it can be seen that the soul is also the seat of the personality and its affections—its inclinations, its capacity for joy or grief, and so forth. Therefore, it is written: *"My soul is exceeding sorrowful"* (Matthew 26:38); *"My soul doth magnify the Lord"* (Luke 1:46); *"Now is my soul troubled"* (John 12:27); *"In your patience possess ye your souls"* (Luke 21:19); *"Vexed his righteous soul"* (2 Peter 2:8); and, *"Beguiling unstable souls"* (v. 14).

It is therefore clear that the soul as well as the body has a certain individual design to it. And this shape of the soul, if I may use the expression, in its capacity for joy, love, grief, patience, and so on, may be filled with a spiritual joy, as the life of the Second Adam is poured out into the vessel of the soul. Or, it may be filled with a soulish joy, which moves into the vessel of the soul from the lower life of the first Adam. In the latter case, the believer, although he is indwelt by the Holy Spirit, is soulish to the degree to which his soul-life is allowed to control these various capacities of the soul. He may cling to a soulish joy and live in the realm of his feelings, which is the seat of his self-consciousness, and not in his spirit, the place of the God-consciousness. In this way, he becomes one of those believers who are always seeking spiritual "experiences" in the sense-consciousness, instead of in the purity of the God-conscious realm alone—in the regenerated human spirit.

The Soul-Life and the Powers of Darkness

But if ye have bitter envying and strife in your hearts, glory not, and lie not against the truth. This wisdom descendeth not from above, but is earthly, sensual, devilish. (James 3:14–15)

I have already referred to this passage, but I quote it now in full in order to show conclusively the relationship of the forces of evil to the soul-life. Here there is no reference to the *"works of the flesh"* (Galatians 5:19) but rather to man's intellectual component, and the words of the text show that evil spirits attack the soulish part of a person as well as his fleshly nature.

It is startling to see the truth put so bluntly and to know that all bitter feelings of envy and rivalry, in connection with the gaining or possession of knowledge, are instigated by evil spirits who attack the soulish life and who have their origin—as Fausset wrote—in hell.

Many true children of God have little or no understanding of this. They may acknowledge satanic influence in the matter of gross sin and the manifestation of the works of the flesh, but not in the realm of what they consider the highest part of civilization—the intellect. Behind this lies an unwillingness to recognize certain statements in the Word of God concerning the Fall, and to admit that fallen man sank utterly into corruption and death, so that even the *"imagination of the thoughts of his heart"*—that is, his mental conceptions—was considered by God to be *"evil continually"* (Genesis 6:5). And behind all this total corruption lies the poison of the Serpent, who gained entrance through the avenue of the desire for wisdom and knowledge (Genesis 3:6).

Evil spirits scheme to thwart the progress of renewal in redeemed believers. This is why it is to their advantage when any element of the fallen life of a believer, whether it is fleshly or soulish, is kept active. They know that as the believer becomes spiritual, his spirit is united more and more with the Lord of Glory, and therefore he is able to escape the power of evil spirits more and more. In addition, he becomes equipped to recognize them and to war against them.

It must be understood that the Fall came about because mankind believed the lie of Satan, and that when Satan succeeded, a poison entered the race of fallen man that runs through every element of his being. This gives Satan the power to access every part of man's tripartite nature. Man's fallen spirit, which is dead to God, is open to the hellish dark world of spirits that are ruled by the Prince of Darkness. His soul—including his intellect, imagination, thoughts, will, and affections—is governed by the life of the first Adam, which is fallen and corrupt. Therefore, his body and soul are completely open to the power of the Poisoner. Because of this, the apostle John bluntly declared that *"the whole world lieth in the evil one"* (1 John 5:19 RV).

Fallen man not only has to be redeemed by the lifeblood of the Son of God, but he also has to be actually transferred from the rule of the power of darkness into the kingdom of God's Son (Colossians 1:13). Every department of his being, beginning with his spirit, must actually be renewed, stage by stage, by deliverance from the power of sin and the soul-life. If the first creation was *"fearfully and wonderfully made"* (Psalm 139:14), then truly the re-creation of man—who had utterly sunk into the soul and the flesh, but who has been lifted again into the realm of spirit to have dominion over soul and body—is a marvelous work that only the triune God could accomplish. The Father gave the Son, the Son gave His life, and the Divine Spirit continually gives Himself with patience and love to accomplish the will of the Trinity.

The reason why the Prince of Darkness resists every step of man's deliverance from his bondage is easy to understand, and it is necessary for us to truly comprehend the elements of the fallen creation that are open to his power. The fact that he fully controls those who are unregenerate is clearly shown in Ephesians 2, where the apostle stated that the *"children of disobedience"* (v. 2), *"fulfilling the desires of the flesh and of the mind"* (v. 3), are wholly dominated by the Enemy. Even when the spirit of a person has been made alive in Christ and has been delivered from the power of sin, his soulish life and elements of his physical body are still open to the influence of evil powers.

A Devilish Soul-Life

In the soulish life of a believer, soulish wisdom becomes *"devilish"* (James 3:15) when evil spirits use it to accomplish their plans. The Enemy can stir up a mental prejudice or preconceived idea—which the person is not aware of—and use it at a critical moment to frustrate the work of the Spirit of God. The way in which the Enemy works through the mind of a believer, even when his heart and spirit are true to God, is a very serious fact in the church of God today, for through the various ideas of good men the Spirit of God is sometimes hindered even more than through the unbelief and hatred of the world. And, again, in the realm of the emotions, the Adversary can stir up the soul-life to such an extent that the deep work of the Spirit of God is quenched and His voice is not heard.

The Adversary can also attack the nervous system and other aspects of a person's physical makeup. In addition, he can use the avenues of the *"works of the flesh"* (Galatians 6:19) and sin in general. These elements are in the very constitution of the human vessel. The powers of darkness are extremely clever at working alongside of or simulating natural conditions, either by influencing a person's temperament or disturbing the functioning of his body. The attack may be in the natural and physical realm, though this is not the real source of the problem. The evil spirits like to manipulate some physical or mental ailment, which serves as a camouflage, or as an excuse, for their activities.

Therefore, the believer should diligently seek spiritual knowledge from God regarding the complex way in which he has been made, so that he may understand himself and know how to act and walk in humble dependence upon the risen Lord for protection from the Evil One. This protection can only operate as the believer looks to the blood of Jesus and, in implicit obedience to His written Word, keeps himself open to all truth that will give him spiritual insight into any possible ground he may have given to evil spirits to attack or gain admittance to his mind or body.

Four

Dividing Soul and Spirit

Dividing Soul and Spirit

*For the word of God is quick, and powerful,
and sharper than any twoedged sword, piercing
even to the dividing asunder of soul and spirit,
and of the joints and marrow, and is a
discerner of the thoughts and intents
of the heart.*
—*Hebrews 4:12*

This remarkable passage in Hebrews clearly sets forth the distinction between soul and spirit, the need for *"dividing"* one from the other, and the means through which this is done so that the believer may become a truly spiritual man and *"live according to God in the spirit"* (1 Peter 4:6). In regard to this passage, Pember pointed out the following:

> [The writer of Hebrews] claims for the Word of God the power of separating, and, as it were, taking to pieces, the

whole being of man, spiritual, psychic
(soulish), and corporeal, even as the
priest flayed and divided limb from limb
the animal for the burnt offering (2
Chronicles 35:11).

Fausset also commented on this passage:

The Word of God is *"living"* and
"powerful"—energetically efficacious
(Greek)...."*Piercing even to the dividing
asunder of soul and spirit"*—that is,
reaching through even to the separation
of the animal soul...from the
spirit...."*And of the joints and marrow"*...distinguishing what is spiritual
from what is carnal and animal in him,
the spirit from the soul....
The Word of God divides the closely
joined parts of man's immaterial being,
soul and spirit.
The clause "[reaching even to] *the
joints and marrow"* is subordinate to
the clause *"even to the dividing asunder
of soul and spirit"*...an image
(appropriate in addressing Jews) from
the literal dividing of joints and pene-
trating to, so as to open out, the marrow
by the priest's knife.

These words show how illustrative and full of teaching this entire passage is to the believer whose eyes are opened to the dangers of permitting his soul-life to dominate him, instead of allowing the Spirit of God to act freely from the sanctuary of his spirit.

A question immediately arises in the believer who desires to be spiritual: "How can I discern what is soulish in my Christian life and service?" The answer is that we are to allow the Lord Jesus to do this for us. The context of the Scripture text for this chapter shows that we are to yield ourselves to our High Priest, who has *"passed into the heavens"* (Hebrews 4:14). *"All things are naked and laid open"* (v. 13 RV) to Christ. In His role as Priest, He will wield the sharp, two-edged sword of His Word, piercing to the point of dividing the soul and spirit within us, discerning even the *"thoughts and intents"* of our hearts. Fausset, in his commentary, wrote that the "Greek [word] for *'thoughts'* refers to the mind and feelings, [and the word] *'intents,'* or rather, 'mental conceptions,' refers to the intellect."

Our High Priest became a man so *"that he might be a merciful and faithful high priest"* (Hebrews 2:17). He is able to sympathize with mankind because He has been touched with the very feeling of our physical and moral weaknesses (Hebrews 4:15, Greek), and He is the only One who can take the sacrificial knife and patiently "divide" the soulish life from its penetration into thoughts and feelings, the intellect, and even mental conceptions. What a work this is! How can the soul-life, which penetrates the very *"joints and marrow,"* be traced and dislodged so that the human spirit, which is indwelt by the Holy Spirit, may dominate, and every thought may be brought *"into captivity...to the obedience of Christ"* (2 Corinthians 10:5)? Our High Priest will not fail or be discouraged in bringing forth victory out of judgment (Matthew 12:20) in all those who commit themselves to His hands and trust Him to wield the knife of His living Word by the Spirit of God.

The Believer's Cooperation with God

However, what is man's part in this process? How is the believer to cooperate with the High Priest in this great and delicate work?

The believer must definitely surrender his entire being as a *"living sacrifice"* (Romans 12:1) upon the altar of the cross. His entire will must be given to God irrevocably, so that the High Priest may, by His Spirit, bring the believer's entire being into conformity to His death (Philippians 3:10). That is, when the Christian yields his will, he is asking Christ to continue working in him until his soulish life is divided from his spirit. In this way, he may become a vessel into which, and through which, the Spirit of God may flow freely from the sanctuary of his spirit.

Next, the believer must continually, persistently, and carefully pray and search the Scriptures. He should pray that the sharp edge of the Word of God may be applied to all that is soulish in his life, and he should implicitly obey the Word to the fullest extent of the understanding that he has been given, according to 1 Peter 1:22: *"Ye have purified your souls in obeying the truth."*

In addition, the believer is to *"deny himself, and take up his cross daily"* (Luke 9:23) amid the circumstances of life, so that he has complete victory over sin and the works of the flesh, while the Spirit of God is doing the more minute work of separating spirit from soul and teaching the believer how to walk according to the Spirit.

The separation of spirit from soul is carried out in the believer who lays himself on the altar (the cross) and trusts the heavenly High Priest to use the sword of His Word as a scalpel to do His "spiritual surgery," and as he obeys Christ's call to *"take up his cross, and follow"* (Matthew 16:24).

The Cross and Soulish Affections

And he that taketh not his cross, and followeth after me, is not worthy of me. He that findeth his life shall lose it: and he that loseth his life for my sake shall find it. (Matthew 10:38–39)

The Revised Version gives the alternate translation for the word *"life"* in the above passage as *soul,* since the Greek noun here is *psuchē.* Jesus made this statement to the Twelve when He sent them out in His name. He warned them that *"a man's foes shall be they of his own household"* (Matthew 10:36). He revealed that if they chose to follow Him first in the path of the cross, it would mean a *"sword"* (v. 34) in their family lives, when the claims of Christ and the family were not in accord. The sword of the Spirit that divides the soulish from the spiritual in the affections is generally manifested in a clash between the

70

known will of God and the wills of loved ones.
Through this experience, the believer is compelled to take up his cross and follow the Lord,
even though it causes conflict with his father
or mother or with his *"own household"*
(Matthew 10:35–36). Fausset wrote:

> We have become so accustomed to
> the expression 'taking up one's cross' in
> the sense of being prepared for tri-
> als...that we are apt to lose sight of its
> primary and proper sense here—a pre-
> paredness to go forth even to crucifixion.

It was the same way with Christ Himself.
He who said, *"Honour thy father and mother"*
(Mark 10:19), also had to say, *"Who is my
mother, or my brethren?"* (Mark 3:33) when his
friends thought He was *"beside himself"* (v. 21)
as He was occupied with His Father's business.
Taking up one's cross in this way and choosing
to make obedience to Christ a priority over
family claims, means such intense suffering to
the natural affections that it is like a sword
piercing the soul. The soul-life is lost through
this process, but the soul now receives true life
as it becomes open to the inflow of the love of
God by the Spirit. In this way, the believer no

longer loves his family members for himself, but
for God, and in and through God.

The lower life is exchanged for the higher.
The soul, in its personality and capacity as a
vessel, remains the same, but it is now ruled
from the spirit by the Spirit of Christ—the
Second Adam—and not merely by the soul-life
of the first Adam (1 Corinthians 15:45–48).

In Luke's gospel, the role of the cross in
dividing spirit and soul in connection with the
soul's affections is more clearly defined, for the
Lord said,

> *If any man come to me, and hate not his
> father, and mother, and wife, and chil-
> dren, and brethren, and sisters, yea, and
> his own life also, he cannot be my disci-
> ple.* (Luke 14:26)

Here again the Greek word for *"life"* is
psuchē—the soul-life.

Matthew's gospel records the test of the
will that Jesus gives to all who want to follow
Him: *"He that loveth father or mother…son or
daughter more than me is not worthy of me"*
(Matthew 10:37). Luke, however, in the above
passage, recorded the language used by the
Lord that describes the *attitude* of the wholly

devoted follower of Christ toward the soul-life and its tendency to permeate the affections—an attitude that is necessary for his purification. Such a believer must *"hate...his own life* [psuchē]*"* (Luke 14:26) when it comes to its penetration into family relationships, so that his soul may be divided from his spirit in this area of his life. In the "hating" and "losing" of his soul-life, he will discover that the higher and purer love and life of Christ will then permeate his close family ties. These were originally ordained and honored by God Himself when He sent His Son to earth in human form, into a human family with human relationships.

The Cross and Soulish Self-Interest

The gospel of Matthew also records a similar statement by the Lord, but this time it was prompted by Peter's words to Him in regard to His own cross. Peter had said, *"Be it far from thee, Lord: this* [death] *shall not be unto thee"* (Matthew 16:22), but the Lord replied that the path of following Him meant that a believer is to *"deny himself"*:

> *If any man will come after me, let him deny himself, and take up his cross, and*

73

> *follow me. For whosoever will save his*
> *life shall lose it: and whosoever will lose*
> *his life for my sake shall find it.*
>   *(Matthew 16:24–25)*

Once again, the word *"life"* in the above passage is the Greek word *psuchē,* and the Revised Version gives *soul* as its alternate translation.

The soul-life is summed up here in the word *"himself,"* when it involves self-centeredness in any form—self-pity, self-interest, shrinking from personal suffering—in short, all that would make a person *"save his life"* rather than go forward in divine strength to pour out his *"soul...unto death"* (Matthew 26:38) for others.

Choosing the path of the cross for Christ's sake means losing one's soul-life in order to gain the pure divine life of Christ. This life of Christ, in its sacrificial nature, is to be poured out through the vessel of the believer's soul for the blessing of the world.

Christ's statement about taking up one's cross is recorded in Mark 8:34–36 with the same words that are used in the gospel of Matthew. The gospel of Luke repeats the statement with the addition of the word *"daily"* (Luke 9:23), showing that the taking up of one's cross, in connection with the outpouring and sacrifice of the soul-life, needs to be a daily choice and bring daily results. It is a distinctly different aspect of the Cross than that given in the book of Romans, especially chapter six, and the other Epistles, where the death of our old nature is acknowledged as a completed fact, made true as the believer considers himself *"dead indeed unto sin, but alive unto God through Jesus Christ our Lord"* (Romans 6:11).

Grasping Earthly Things

Remember Lot's wife. Whosoever shall seek to gain his life [soul, RV, mg] *shall lose it; and whosoever shall lose his life* [soul, RV, mg] *shall preserve it.*
(Luke 17:32–33)

In this passage from Luke, we find the same emphatic words repeated by the Lord in connection with self-interest, the natural instinct of self-preservation, and the grasping of earthly possessions. *"Remember Lot's wife,"* said the Lord Jesus as He pointed out the natural tendency of the soul-life to turn back in a time of danger in order to save possessions rather than letting them go.

Here is the law of gaining the higher life of the spirit: lose in order to gain. The soulish life seeks earthly treasures, but this tendency must be renounced. Again, the dividing of soul and spirit will come about through the attitude of the believer when he is tested by the daily circumstances of life—circumstances that are both favorable and unfavorable. The Bible tells us that some believers who underwent trials *"took joyfully the spoiling of* [their] *goods"* (Hebrews 10:34). This attitude toward possessions is sometimes a greater manifestation of divine grace than the sacrifice of one's life.

Renouncing the soul-life, with its inherent clinging to the things of earth, is necessary for gaining the life of Christ, which brings such an assurance of abundance in God that earth's treasures become of very little worth and are easily forsaken in the times of testing that come to all men. It often takes a crisis in our lives to show us where true life may be found.

The undue absorption of the children of God with houses and other possessions, to the neglect of the kingdom of God, is clearly an aspect of the soul-life. This clinging, or preoccupation with necessary earthly concerns, requires the surgery of the Great High Priest in the dividing of soul and spirit, so that the affections of His blood-bought ones may be set on things above (Colossians 3:2).

Self-Love

> *He that loveth his life* [soul, RV, mg]
> *shall lose it; and he that hateth his life*
> [soul, RV, mg] *in this world shall keep it*
> *unto life eternal.*   *(John 12:25)*

The Greek word for *"life"* in *"life eternal"* is different from the other word for *"life"* in this verse, which is *psuchē,* or *soul.* "Life eternal" is *zoe,* and refers to the higher spiritual life. The contrast between the soul-life and the higher life of the spirit is very clearly presented in this passage. The soul-life is defined here as self-love: *"He that loveth his* [soul]," which simply means himself. We have seen that the soul-life penetrates family relationships and is manifested in self-pity, self-protection, and a grasping of the possessions of earth. In brief, it is summed up in "my family," "myself," and "my possessions"—with self-love permeating everything.

All this, the Master says, means loss—eternal loss—for it comes from the life derived from the first Adam, is manifested through the personality of the soul, and prevents the soul from being dominated by the spirit and giving expression to the pure divine life of the Second Adam.

Is it sinful to hold onto this self-love? Yes, when the light comes and we see the truth. In a deeper sense, the soul-life is a manifestation of sin—although unknown sin—for the entire life of our *"natural man"* (1 Corinthians 2:14) has been poisoned by sin. The soulish life has been tainted, and even in those who understand that they are dead to sin, as the Bible clearly teaches in Romans 6, and who therefore cease to walk according to the flesh (Romans 8:1) and to manifest the works of the flesh (Galatians 5:19), it penetrates into the realm of the affections. Its subtle appearance in self-love, self-pity, grasping for possessions, and other aspects of self-centeredness must be called sin, even though it manifests itself in less recognizable ways, since it works through the intellect, emotions, and affections.

The Pathway of Freedom

For the love of Christ constraineth us; because we thus judge, that if one died for all, then were all dead: and that he died for all, that they which live should

*not henceforth live unto themselves, but
unto him which died for them, and rose
again.* (2 *Corinthians 5:14–15*)

The work of dividing spirit and soul is per-
formed by the Lord Himself, as His Spirit
wields the Word of God as a living, active
sword that penetrates to the inmost recesses of
the immaterial being of man.

But we have our part to do. The Spirit of
God cannot carry out His work without the
believer's consent and cooperation. Here is a
brief summary of how the believer must cooperate with God:

1. The believer must see the necessity of dividing soul and spirit and, as his sacrifice is
   laid on the altar, he must definitely consent
   to the work being done in him.

2. The believer must consistently place his will
   on God's side in the day-to-day working out
   of the dividing of his soul and spirit, as the
   circumstances of life require it.

3. The basis of the way of the cross, as it is
   presented in Romans 6:1–14, must be af-
   firmed continually. As the believer now

79

considers himself *"dead indeed unto sin"* (v. 11) and actively carries out the command not to let sin reign in his mortal body, finding that his flesh is *"crucified...with* [its] *affections and lusts"* (Galatians 5:24), he must also consider himself dead to sin in its more subtle forms, which are evident through the soul-life: the evil attitudes of self, such as inordinate self-love, self-pity, and similar self-centeredness.

4. The believer who fulfills these conditions must now carry out in practice his new spiritual understanding, purpose, and faith; he must continually be faithful to all that he is shown by the Spirit of God. He must deliberately refuse all intrusion of the evil tendencies of the soul-life and choose to open himself to the higher life of Christ in his spirit.

5. The believer must seek in all things to walk according to the Spirit; to discern what is spirit and what is soul, so that he may follow the one and refuse the other; and to

understand the laws of the spirit-life in order to walk in them and become a true spiritual Christian.

As the believer fulfills these conditions, he will find that he truly becomes a new creation in Christ. As the sword of the Spirit is wielded by the hands of the heavenly High Priest, piercing to the dividing of soul and spirit, the power of the cross becomes evident. It traces the soul-life even to the joints and marrow, to the inner recesses of the soul in the source of its activity and the very core of its affections. More than this, it even discerns the influence of the soulish life in the feelings and in the very thoughts and ideas of the mind. Now the believer more and more joyfully and easily walks according to the written Word of God, and takes up his cross as it is brought to bear upon him daily in the providence of God.

As the believer comprehends, with ever increasing clarity, the fact of his death with Christ, his spirit is divided more and more from his soul and is joined in essential union with the risen Lord, who is a *"life-giving spirit"* (1 Corinthians 15:45 RV). In this way, he becomes *"one spirit"* (1 Corinthians 6:17) with Christ, and his human spirit becomes a channel through which the Spirit of Christ may flow to a needy world.

Five

Laws of the Spirit-Life

Laws of the Spirit-Life

And the very God of peace sanctify you wholly;
and I pray God your whole spirit and soul and
body be preserved blameless unto the coming of
our Lord Jesus Christ.
        —1 Thessalonians 5:23

As I wrote earlier, the above passage in Thessalonians is one of only two verses found in English language versions of the Bible that plainly declares the tripartite nature of man. This verse describes the three aspects of the nature of man in their proper relationship to one another—the way God created them to be. It is remarkable how frequently the order is changed by many believers when they quote this verse; they pray that they may be sanctified "body, soul, and spirit," which is in the opposite order. This shows that the mind unconsciously communicates the true

85

condition of the fallen creation. Yet, when a Christian is illuminated by the Spirit of God, his spirit is brought back to its place of control over his mind as well as all his other faculties.

The apostle Paul, in his prayer for the Thessalonians, gave a comprehensive picture of the spiritual Christian. His highest desire for these believers was that they might be completely sanctified. He also wrote about this to the Colossians, stating that the reason he worked so hard was so that he might present every believer fully mature, or *"perfect in Christ Jesus"* (Colossians 1:28). According to a noted biblical scholar, the word *"perfect"* here denotes "grown to the ripeness of maturity." *"I pray God,"* Paul said, *"your whole spirit and soul and body be preserved blameless."* Being *"preserved blameless"* comes after being sanctified wholly.

What does being perfect in Christ mean for each part of man's tripartite nature?

Regarding the spirit, the triune God, who is Spirit (John 4:24), takes up residence in the spirit of a believer, who is first regenerated in his spirit by the Holy Spirit through the redemptive work of the Son.

Regarding the soul, as the triune God dwells in the spirit of a believer, He manifests

Himself through the vessel of the believer's personality: the believer's will is completely one with the will of God, his intellect is renewed and illuminated by the Holy Spirit, and his emotions are under his total control and use, yet are guided by the Spirit of God.

Regarding the body, as the triune God dwells in the spirit of a believer and manifests Himself through the avenue of his soul, He keeps the believer's body under complete control (1 Corinthians 9:27); every part of the body yields quick obedience as an *"instrument of righteousness"* (Romans 6:13). In this way, the outer man—the body—truly becomes a sanctuary of the Holy Spirit (1 Corinthians 6:19).

This is a picture of the spiritual believer who has grown to the "ripeness of maturity"; who is completely sanctified in spirit, soul, and body; and who needs to be *"preserved blameless"* by having the God of Peace dwell in the center of his being.

From Soulish to Spiritual

But how does the believer progress from the soulish stage to become a truly spiritual Christian? Fausset wrote, "The 'spiritual' is the man distinguished above his fellowmen as he in whom the spirit rules." This authority of the spirit not only refers to the Spirit of God Himself ruling over the carnal or soulish man, but also to the human spirit ruling over the soul and body as it is indwelt and strengthened by the Holy Spirit. This is what Paul prayed for regarding the Ephesians: that they might be *"strengthened with might by the Spirit in the inner man"* (Ephesians 3:16)—or, as Bishop Moule put it, in the "regenerate human spirit."

Spiritual believers are those who walk according to the Spirit and who are in agreement with the Spirit. Their spirits cooperate with the Holy Spirit in such a way that the *"life-giving spirit"* (1 Corinthians 15:45 RV) of the Second Adam is able to freely and fully bring alive the faculties of the soul (mind, imagination, reason, judgment), give life to the members of the body, and manifest through them His fullest and highest will.

For this to come about, believers must understand two ways in which God works in them. First, we learn from Hebrews 4:12 that the Word of God divides soul from spirit. Secondly, we discover from 1 Thessalonians 5:23 that the God of Peace sanctifies us completely by taking possession of and working through our spirits and by seeing that our souls and bodies fulfill their proper functions.

The apostle Paul wrote, *"He that is joined unto the Lord is one spirit"* (1 Corinthians 6:17), and, *"Ye also are become dead to the law by the body of Christ; that ye should be married to another, even to him who is raised from the dead"* (Romans 7:4). This clearly describes the "marriage," or union with Christ in the spirit, that is the purpose and outcome of the work of the Cross. This union with the risen and ascended Lord can only occur in a person's spirit and can only be experienced as the spirit of the believer is separated from the entanglement of the soul. For, as one theologian observed, the risen Lord is not the Bridegroom of the soul but of the spirit. The soul—the personality— can only be the vessel through which the Lord manifests His own life, bringing forth, in union with the believer's spirit, *"fruit unto God"* (Romans 7:4).

A spiritual person, therefore, is one in whom, through the dividing of soul and spirit by the Word of God, the spirit has been freed from the entanglement of the soul. As the eighteenth century theologian Bromley said, the spirit is raised out of the soul's "embrace"

and joined to the Lord in a union of essence—
spirit with Spirit. In this way, the believer's
soul and body may serve as vehicles for the expression of the will and life and love of the
Lord Himself.

In light of this, the contrast between the
works of the flesh and the fruit of the Spirit,
described in Galatians 5:19–23, is very striking. The flesh is active within us, and it brings
its repulsive manifestations to the surface of
our lives. However, the believer who understands that he is dead to sin, that his flesh has
been crucified, and that his soul has been divided from his spirit by the Word of God, is
united to the Lord. This union brings forth
fruit—spontaneous manifestations of life—and
this fruit is revealed in and through the soul in
its various forms: *"love, joy, peace, longsuffer-
ing, gentleness, goodness, faith, meekness, tem-
perance* [self-control, RV, mg]" (vv. 22–23).

The inclusion of self-control as a fruit of
the Spirit shows that the Spirit of God uses the
"self"—the personality or soul of a person—as
His means of control. The personality, defined
in this way, is therefore not to be destroyed or
suppressed, but ennobled as it becomes a vehicle for expressing the Spirit of Christ dwelling
within. The fruit of the Spirit is manifested

through the soul, but it does not originate there. Instead, it comes from the Holy Spirit, who works through the human spirit.

There are many passages in the Scriptures that describe the various activities of the soul, which derives its life from the spirit. We read of being *"fervent in spirit"* (Romans 12:11); *"purpos*[ing] *in the spirit"* (Acts 19:21); the *"spirit of faith"* (2 Corinthians 4:13); *"love in the Spirit"* (Colossians 1:8). All these activities are manifested through the avenue of the soul: wisdom through the mind, purposing through the will, love through the affections, joy through the emotions. However, they spring from the eternal depth of the spirit and not merely from the senses alone.

Laws of the Spirit

When a believer is learning how to cooperate with God in restoring his spirit to the place of authority it should have, it is vitally important that he learn the laws governing the life of the spirit, and how to walk according to his spirit. If he does not, he may fail to cooperate with the Holy Spirit and may give opportunities to deceiving spirits of Satan to ensnare him with counterfeits of the true life of the spirit. These counterfeits are produced in the realm of the soul, and many believers do not recognize that they are false, for the objective of the deceiving spirits is to cause the believer to unknowingly walk in the realm of the soul again.

To review, the spiritual believer, whose spirit has been liberated or divided from his soul—is one who is governed by his spirit, and not by his soul or body. However, this does not mean that he cannot be entangled in the life of the soul again if, through an ignorance of the laws of the spirit, he fails to let the spirit rule. He must know how to discern whether he is experiencing something from the spirit, the soul, or the body; how to keep his spirit free and open to the Spirit of God; and how he can keep his spirit in continuous cooperation with the Holy Spirit.

He also needs to be able to recognize and deal with attacks from evil spirits that seek to get believers' spirits out of fellowship with God. These evil spirits may cause him to live in the realm of his soul again. They may paralyze the activity of his spirit and cause it to be passive, or, on the contrary, drive it to excessive activity. They do all these things with the purpose of preventing or hindering believers from continually resisting their attacks and from waging spiritual warfare against their evil schemes.

In order to walk in the realm of the spirit, a believer must know what is coming from his own spirit and how to listen to the demands of his spirit rather than quenching them. For example, suppose a feeling of heaviness comes on his spirit, but he goes on working, putting up with the pressure. He finds it hard to work, but he has no time to investigate the reason for the heaviness. At last the weight becomes unendurable, and he is forced to stop and see what is the matter. He should have paid attention to the claims of his spirit when he first felt them; then, in a brief prayer, he could have taken the weight to God and refused all pressure from the Enemy.

He must also be able to read his spirit and know at once when it is no longer cooperating with the Holy Spirit, quickly refusing all attacks that are drawing his spirit out of its stability of fellowship with God. Moreover, he should know when his spirit is being influenced by the poison of evil spirits. For example, he should recognize the injection of sadness, irritability, complaining, grumbling, faultfinding, touchiness, bitterness, hurt feelings, jealousy, and so on, when they come directly from the Enemy to his spirit. He should resist all sadness, gloom, and grumbling that are introduced into his spirit, for the victorious life of a freed spirit means joyfulness. This intrusion of various feelings and emotions is not the manifestation of the works of the flesh, when the believer is one who understands what it means to live according to his spirit. However, it will quickly reach the sphere of the flesh if it is not recognized and dealt with through sharp refusal and resistance.

In addition, a believer should know when his spirit is in the proper position of control over his soul and body, and yet not driven beyond due measure by the demands of spiritual conflict or environment. There are three conditions of the spirit that the believer should be able to discern and deal with: when his spirit is depressed or "down"; when his spirit is in its proper position, composed and in calm control; and when the peace of his spirit has been disrupted, that is, when he is feeling strained or driven. When a believer is familiar with walking according to his spirit, and discerns that his spirit is not in its proper position, he knows how to lift it out of its depression or how to stop, by a quiet act of his will, any overactivity, when his soul becomes disturbed by his own overeagerness or by the drive of spiritual foes.

If a person's spirit is in contact with the Spirit of God, it is full of light; apart from Him it is darkness. When the spirit is indwelt by Him, *"the spirit of man is the candle of the LORD"* (Proverbs 20:27). But when the spirit is bound or in heaviness, it ceases to function or to be the source of power and energy in a believer's life. If a person feels a heaviness in his spirit, he should find out what the weight is. If he were to be asked, "Is it your body?" he would probably reply that it was not, but would add that he felt bound inside. Then, what is it that is "bound" or "weighted"? Is it not his spirit? One's spirit can be bound or free, and the possibilities and potentialities of the human spirit can only be known when the spirit is joined to Christ and, through experience, is made strong by the Holy Spirit to *"stand against the wiles of the devil"* (Ephesians 6:11).

Six

The
Spiritual
Christian

The Spiritual Christian

He that is spiritual judgeth all things.
—1 Corinthians 2:15

In Paul's first letter to the Corinthians, he drew a striking contrast between the spiritual and the carnal believer. The spiritual believer was described by the apostle as *"perfect"* (1 Corinthians 2:6), that is, "full-grown" (v. 6 RV, mg) in Christ. The carnal believer can only be fed with *"milk"* (1 Corinthians 3:2), the simplest element of the Gospel. Yet the mature or spiritual believer can receive the *"deep things of God"* (1 Corinthians 2:10), things that cannot even be spoken *"in words which man's wisdom teacheth, but which the Spirit teacheth; comparing spiritual things with spiritual* [interpreting spiritual things to spiritual men, RV, mg]*"* (v. 13 RV).

Note that, in this instance, the Scriptures reveal that the Holy Spirit teaches *"spiritual things,"* such as facts—not truths, but things that are as real as what is material on earth. Moreover, the apostle made it clear that a person who is *"natural"* or soulish cannot receive the *"things of the Spirit"* (1 Corinthians 2:14) any more than fleshly *"babes in Christ"* (1 Corinthians 3:1) can, for to the soulish intellect and wisdom they appear to be nothing but foolishness.

Spiritual things can be examined just as well as material things. Yet none except those who are spiritual can discern, or examine (1 Corinthians 2:14 RV, mg), the things of the Spirit. The spiritual man examines all things (v. 15 RV, mg) for he is able, by the Spirit, to penetrate to the inner spiritual source of these things and to pierce through the veil of sight and sense to the spiritual truths lying behind it. However, the soulish believer cannot perceive anything beyond the point that his intellect can take him. He can examine all things in the natural sphere, but nothing else.

To paraphrase the apostle Paul, "The spiritual man is ripe in understanding" (1 Corinthians 2:15). If we carefully examine all the references in Paul's epistles to the

"perfect" or *"complete"* believer, we will see
that the requirement for reaching the spiritual
stage, or the stage of full growth and maturity
in Christ, is having one's soul and spirit divided by the sword of the Spirit. The mature
stage is continually associated with the knowledge, teaching, and discernment of spiritual
things. All of these have to do with the soul,
which needs to be purged of the soulish life so
that the mind may be able to receive the spiritual wisdom that is one of the characteristics
of the spiritual believer.

For example, the apostle Paul wrote in his
letters:

> *We speak wisdom among the perfect*
> [full-grown, RV, mg].
> *(1 Corinthians 2:6 RV)*

> *Teaching every man in all wisdom; that
> we may present every man perfect* [same
> Greek word as above] *in Christ Jesus.*
> *(Colossians 1:28)*

> *Be not children in mind…but in mind be
> men* [of full age, RV, mg].
> *(1 Corinthians 14:20 RV)*

Solid food is for full-grown men, even those who by reason of use have their senses exercised to discern good and evil.
(Hebrews 5:14 RV)

Let us therefore, as many as be perfect, be thus minded. *(Philippians 3:15)*

In the last verse, the word *"perfect"* means "ripe in understanding." *"Perfect"* is the antithesis of *"babes in Christ"* used in 1 Corinthians 3:1, and is the same Greek word as *"full-grown"* used in Hebrews 5:14 (RV).

Paul prayed that the Colossians *"might be filled with the knowledge of his will in all wisdom and spiritual understanding"* (Colossians 1:9). In a practical example of the importance of this knowledge, Paul wrote to the Galatians that it should be a spiritual believer who restores a brother who is overtaken in sin, for only he can exercise the heavenly wisdom required for faithfulness in dealing with the sin from the standpoint of God, while tenderly loving the erring brother (Galatians 6:1).

The apostle also wrote to the Ephesians,

Till we all attain unto the unity of the faith, and of the knowledge of the Son of

*God, unto a full-grown man, unto the
measure of the stature of the fulness of
Christ.   (Ephesians 4:13 RV)*

Here again knowledge is linked with full
growth and the fullness of Christ. *"The unity
of the faith"* that should characterize the body
of Christ and bring about its full stature cannot be manifested until each of the individual
members reaches the stage of maturity and
becomes a spiritual believer. Again, each
member cannot become spiritual until ho
knows the separation of soul and spirit—so
that his spirit may be fully joined to the risen
Lord—and until the vessel of his soul, in its
intellectual and other departments, is ener-
gized and dominated by the spirit and not by
the lower life of the first Adam.

Made Perfect in Love

The word *"perfect"* (1 Corinthians 2:6),
which is alternately translated "full-grown" in
the marginal note of the Revised Version, is
often connected with the mind or knowledge
by the apostle Paul. However, it is joined with
the concept of love by the apostle John. He
spoke of the believer being *"made perfect in*

love" (1 John 4:18). He tells how *"perfect love casteth out fear"* (v. 18) and how *"love made perfect"* gives *"boldness in the day of judgment"* (v. 17). The first epistle of John depicts the spiritual believer, therefore, as one whose affections of the soul are possessed with the love of God so completely that they are entirely filled with the love that flows from Him, as He dwells in the spirit. *"God dwelleth in us, and his love is perfected in us"* (v. 12), wrote the Beloved Apostle. In other words, the vessel of the soul is perfectly filled with divine love, so that, up to its measure and capacity, it is complete with the love of God. It is so full of love that there is no room for fear.

But John's words mean even more than the fact that the divine love of God, who dwells in the spirit of the believer, can flow freely through the vessel of the soul. He is really describing what it means to live by one's spirit as it is ruled by the Spirit of God—to live in the sphere of the God-consciousness. He wrote, *"God is love; and he that dwelleth in love dwelleth in God, and God in him"* (1 John 4:16). The spiritual believer who lives and walks in a spirit of love is therefore dwelling in God. If fear or hate comes in, he has descended to the realm of the soul, or, through the attack of evil spirits, has lost his ability to cooperate with God in his spirit. When he discerns this, he must immediately go to Christ and submit himself to the dividing of his soul and spirit. At the same time, he must acknowledge to God that he has sinned and seek the application of the cleansing blood of Christ, according to 1 John 1:7, 9. And, he must resist the powers of darkness and once more take up the *"whole armour of God"* (Ephesians 6:11) for victory.

Oneness with All Believers

The spiritual believer is perfected into one spirit with those who are in Christ. The word *"perfect"* used in 1 Corinthians 2:6 was also used by the Lord Jesus, in His High Priestly Prayer in John 17, to describe the union between His redeemed ones. This was the burden on His heart on the evening before He went to the cross to make that union possible:

> *As thou, Father, art in me, and I in thee, that they also may be one in us...that they may be one, even as we are one: I in them, and thou in me, that they may be made perfect in one.* (John 17:21–23)

The essential union that exists between Father and Son is the same type of union that the Christian has with other believers: the union of spirit with spirit. The language of the Lord is unmistakable. He said, *"That they may be one, even as we are one."* This means Father and Son dwelling in the spirit of the believer, by the Holy Spirit, in perfect union; and, according to Christ's own words, it also means the same union of spirit with other believers. The spiritual believer is therefore not only one with Christ in God, who is love, but he also finds the same union with the same God abiding in others. Therefore, he cannot be fully abiding in God if he, to any degree, succumbs to the life of the soul that is manifested in divisions, partiality, or partisanship.

Walking in the Light

Again, it is of the spiritual believer that the apostle John wrote:

If we walk in the light, as he is in the light, we have fellowship one with another, and the blood of Jesus Christ his Son cleanseth us from all sin.

(1 John 1:7)

106

Walking in the light can only be done by the believer who is living in the sphere of the God-consciousness, where God dwells in his spirit. Any descent into the realm of the soul may be compared to the spirit—which is joined to Him who is *"the true Light"* (John 1:9)—sinking into an opaque vessel, which obscures the light. But when the believer abides in God, he remains and walks in light, and in that light he finds fellowship with God and with others who dwell in light. At the same time, the blood of Jesus continuously cleanses him from all unknown sin that may unconsciously touch him through any intrusion of the soul-life or through contact with sin in the surrounding world.

"God is light, and in him is no darkness at all" (1 John 1:5). *"He that loveth...abideth in the light"* (1 John 2:10). This is the ascension life, or the life *"hid with Christ in God"* (Colossians 3:3), of which the apostle Paul wrote. It was spoken of to the disciples by the Lord Jesus in His farewell words in the Upper Room at Jerusalem, but this life was brought into their real experience by the Holy Spirit on the Day of Pentecost. At that time, the Spirit of the glorified Jesus entered their spirits, and they were lifted up out of the realm of the soul into spiritual oneness with the glorified Lord.

107

As they dwelt in Him and He in them (1 John 4:15–16), the world believed. It saw the oneness of the Spirit-filled believers *"made perfect in love"* (v. 18), with all fear cast out; it saw Jesus' followers walking in light to such an extent that sinful selfishness, such as that manifested by Ananias (Acts 5:1–5), could not be allowed to exist among them.

In view of all this, and what it means to Christ and His church that all the members of His body should become spiritual and perfected into their place of union with the risen Head, the importance of the believer understanding the difference between *soul* and *spirit* cannot be overestimated. On his ability to cease living according to the flesh in the sense-consciousness, and according to the soul in the self-consciousness, rests his ability to grow into a fully spiritual believer. Only in this way does the believer become one who is able to understand his spirit and to discern and examine spiritual things; one who is sanctified wholly by the complete liberation of his spirit from the domination of either soul or body, and who is indwelt by the triune God; and one who, walking *"whereto* [he has] *already attained"* (Philippians 3:16), is pressing on to fuller completion in Christ.

It is hard to determine how long the stage between the first step of the new birth and being full-grown in the life of Christ should last. However, the language used by the apostle to the Corinthians, and again by the writer to the Hebrews, suggests blame that many had continued too long in the stage of babyhood and needed spiritual milk because of their weak spiritual lives, when they should have been teachers (Hebrews 5:12–13), leading other *"babes"* (1 Corinthians 3:1) on into full growth. The baby stage can evidently be extended or shortened, and it does not need to be measured by ordinary periods of time. It is probably determined by the amount of truth a believer understands and receives, as well as his spiritual knowledge and yieldedness.

In any event, the language of the writer to the Hebrews makes it clear that the attitude of the believer has much to do with his progress. Writing to those he had just rebuked by saying that they had become *"dull of hearing"* (Hebrews 5:11) and needed to be taught again the first principles of the Gospel, he said: *"Wherefore let us cease to speak of the first principles of Christ, and press on unto* [full growth, RV, mg]*"* (Hebrews 6:1 RV). These are almost the very words that Paul wrote in the third chapter of Philippians, where he told of his own eager pressing on. He did not consider himself to be *"already perfect"* (Philippians 3:12), although he could write, *"Let us therefore, as many as be perfect,"* that is, complete or fully mature, *"be thus minded"* (v. 15) in pressing on toward the goal of the upward calling of God in Christ Jesus (v. 14).

The Spiritual Man and the Spiritual Body

The *"spiritual body"* referred to in 1 Corinthians 15:44, with which the believer will be clothed in the resurrection, is a logical outcome of the spiritual stage we have been considering. The apostle Paul wrote, *"That was not first which is spiritual, but that which is natural; and afterward that which is spiritual"* (v. 46).

The babe in Christ is still carnal (1 Corinthians 3:3), but by taking hold of the truth of Romans 6, he ceases to walk according to the flesh and walks according to the Spirit. Then he comprehends the dividing of soul and spirit and becomes a spiritual believer. His mind is renewed, and his soul and body are a vehicle through which God may express Himself. The original order of the tripartite man is restored: the Holy Spirit rules in the liberated spirit (the

seat of the God-consciousness), with the soul—
or personality—as the vessel (the seat of the self-
consciousness), and the body as the slave (the
seat of the sense-consciousness).

At this point, the believer is truly spiritual. Or, to put it very simply, we might say
that he is a spirit dwelling in the vessel of the
soul, which is encased in a physical, mortal
body. The language of Paul clearly shows that
the full redemption of the body will not come
about until the appearing of the Lord from
heaven:

> *We ourselves groan within ourselves,
> waiting for the adoption, to wit, the re-
> demption of our body.   (Romans 8:23)*

> *We look for the Saviour, the Lord Jesus
> Christ: who shall change our vile body,
> that it may be fashioned like unto his
> glorious body.   (Philippians 3:20–21)*

> *For we that are in this tabernacle do
> groan, being burdened: not for that we
> would be unclothed, but clothed upon,
> that mortality might be swallowed up of
> life.   (2 Corinthians 5:4)*

The body is, therefore, still a *"natural body"* (1 Corinthians 15:44), a mortal body (Romans 8:11), a vessel of clay (2 Corinthians 4:7), and not until it is sown in the earth at death will it be raised a *"spiritual body"* (1 Corinthians 15:44). Or, it will be changed into a spiritual body in *"the twinkling of an eye"* (v. 52) at the Lord's coming.

Yet, the spiritual believer who lives under the control of the Spirit day by day may have an increasing pledge of the coming redemption of his body, for as he walks in the Spirit, his body shares in the life-giving power of the Spirit. This is according to Romans, where the apostle declared,

> *If the Spirit of him that raised up Jesus from the dead dwell in you, he that raised up Christ from the dead shall also quicken your mortal bodies by his Spirit that dwelleth in you.*
> *(Romans 8:11)*

The full power of the reality of this quickening of the mortal body, by the same Spirit of the Father that raised Jesus from the dead, can be known only as far as a believer's soullife is continuously lost by the power of the

112

cross (Matthew 16:24–25). For the mortal body can only be quickened by the Holy Spirit when the *"life-giving spirit"* (1 Corinthians 15:45 RV) is free to energize soul and body.

The apostle's words in 2 Corinthians 4:10–12 have to do with this stage of the believer's life. Just as the soul-life has to be lost in order for a person to find the life of the Spirit flowing through his soul and its faculties, so the same principle of loss for gain must work in the mortal body. Therefore, it is written: *"Always bearing about in the body the dying of the Lord Jesus, that the life also of Jesus might be made manifest in our body"* (2 Corinthians 4:10).

The loss of the soul-life animating the soul is gradual; it gives way to the inflow of the life of the Spirit as the believer yields to the dividing of soul and spirit, brought about by the wielding of the sword of the Spirit by the heavenly High Priest. In the same way, the *"dying of the Lord Jesus"* in the mortal body is gradually brought about, as the believer follows on in the way of the cross, *"troubled," "perplexed," "persecuted," "cast down"* (2 Corinthians 4:8–9)—more than that, as he is *"pressed out of measure, above strength, insomuch that* [he despairs] *even of life"* (2 Corinthians 1:8). This

113

casts him upon the God who raises the dead (v. 9) and reveals the life of Jesus in him, manifested in the renewal and sustaining of his mortal body.

This losing of one's life to gain the life of Jesus is carried on by the will of God, as the spiritual believer follows on to know the Lord:

> *For we which live are alway delivered unto death for Jesus' sake, that the life also of Jesus might be made manifest in our mortal flesh. So then death worketh in us, but life in you.*
>
> *(2 Corinthians 4:11–12)*

Painful as it is to the *"mortal flesh,"* the spiritual believer, when he is able to examine these deep things of God, can see that the working out of the death and life of Christ in a believer means two results of vital importance to the Lord and His people.

First, when the life of Jesus can freely flow from a believer's spirit through the faculties of his soul, and when it brings life to his mortal body with unhindered power, it means life to others as well as to the believer himself—a renewed life to the whole church of

Christ, as depicted by the Lord in His promise of *"rivers of living water"* (John 7:38).

Next, this renewal of the mortal body is the *"earnest of the Spirit"* (2 Corinthians 5:5), by which the body itself is being prepared for the hour when *"that mortality might be swallowed up of life"* (v. 4). As the apostle wrote, *"He that hath wrought us for the selfsame thing is God, who also hath given unto us the earnest of the Spirit"* (v. 5).

Some Dangers Facing the Spiritual Man

The believer who has become truly spiritual is not removed from the realm of conflict; rather, he enters into a more subtle phase of it, as is outlined in Ephesians 6:10–18. The believer who is seated *"in heavenly places in Christ Jesus"* (Ephesians 2:6) is afterward described as wrestling with *"spiritual wickedness in high places"* (Ephesians 6:12), particularly in the form of the *"wiles of the devil"* (v. 11).

This indicates that in the conflict in which the spiritual believer is engaged, he mainly needs to watch against the subtle, spiritual deception of supernatural foes, who are seeking to entangle him in matters connected with the spiritual realm, rather than in the conflict between flesh and spirit described in Galatians 5.

In this phase of conflict, the strategies of the powers of darkness are mainly directed toward getting the spiritual man to walk, in some degree, according to his soul and not according to his spirit; that is, to be influenced by and to walk by anything in the realm of his senses, rather than allowing his spirit alone to lead, in cooperation with the Holy Spirit of God.

It is essential, then, that the spiritual believer should understand that evil spirits of Satan can create a counterfeit of the human spirit in the realm of the soul. They do this by getting access to the outer man by deceitful means, and then producing feelings in the person that do not come from his spirit. When these feelings—which may *appear* spiritual—get a hold, they may become strong enough to silence or overpower the true activity of the person's spirit or his true spiritual feelings. If the believer is ignorant of the tactics of the Enemy in this way, his spirit will easily sink into disuse because he will follow the counterfeit spiritual feelings, thinking that he is walking according to the Spirit.

When the true activity of the believer's spirit ceases, the evil spirits may suggest to him that God is now guiding through the renewed mind (Romans 12:2). This is an attempt to hide their counterfeit activities and the fact that the believer is no longer being controlled by his spirit. At the same time, counterfeit spiritual knowledge will be introduced to his mind, followed by counterfeit reasoning, judgment, and the like. The believer will think that he has received spiritual insight from God because he is unaware that he has ceased to walk according to his spirit and is now walking according to his mind and body.

Another danger that the spiritual believer faces is the subtle attempt of demonic spirits to get him to walk according to the flesh by creating physical sensations in his body that he thinks are spiritual. To defeat this deception, a believer should understand that all physical consciousness of supernatural things, and even undue physical consciousness of natural things, should be refused, since both distract the mind from walking according to the spirit and cause it to focus on bodily sensations. Undue physical consciousness is also an obstacle to a person's ability to keep his concentration; in a spiritual believer, the Enemy's attack on his physical consciousness may also break the concentration of his mind and bring a cloud upon his spirit. Therefore, he should keep his body calm and under full control. Hysterical laughter and any other impulsive behavior that arouses the physical life, to the extent of dominating mind and spirit, should be avoided. Believers who desire to be spiritual and of *"full age"* (Hebrews 5:14) in the life of God must avoid excess, extravagance, and extremes in all things (1 Corinthians 9:25–27).

When a believer allows the physical realm to dominate him and misunderstands the supernatural experiences that he feels in his body, his body does the work of his spirit and is forced into a prominence that suppresses the true life of the spirit. Under such conditions, the body feels the pressure and feels the conflict, thus becoming the person's "sense" in place of his mind and spirit. A believer should learn to distinguish between the different realms of his life and know how to discern the true feelings of his spirit, which are neither emotional (soulish) nor physical. For example, the Bible reveals that we may be *"troubled in spirit"* (John 13:21) and *"pressed in the spirit"* (Acts 18:5).

Through ignorance, a large majority of believers walk according to their souls—that is, their minds and emotions—under the impression that they are walking according to their spirits. Because of what this means (it deprives believers of vital spiritual power), satanic forces use all the deception at their disposal to draw them to live in the realm of their souls or bodies, sometimes flashing visions to their minds, making presentations to their minds during prayer, or giving exquisite sensations of joy or buoyancy of life to their bodies.

When a believer depends upon supernatural experiences that come from outside of him or upon experiences in the sense realm, this blocks his inward spiritual life that is meant to be controlled by the Spirit. Through the bait of "experiences" in the senses, the believer is drawn to live in the outer man of his body, instead of living in the true sphere of his spirit. Then, when he ceases to act from his spirit in the center of his being, he is caught by the external workings of evil supernatural beings, and he loses—quite unconsciously—his internal cooperation with God. Then his spirit, which is the organ of the Holy Spirit in warfare against spiritual foes, drops into dormancy and is ignored, because the believer is occupied with his sensory experiences. Consequently, his spirit is practically useless, either for guidance, power in service, or conflict.

Finally, there is a serious danger that arises when the human spirit acts apart from cooperation with the Holy Spirit. When the spirit has been divided from the soul and has become dominant, it is then open to being influenced by deceiving spirits in quite another way. Suppose that, in one of the ways already indicated or otherwise, a person has unknowingly ceased to cooperate with the Holy Spirit, but is still guided by his spirit. He is liable to think that his own masterful spirit is reflecting the power of God, because in other ways he sees the Holy Spirit using him in winning souls. Under that delusion, a flood of indignation may be inserted into his spirit, which he pours out, thinking it is all from God. Others, however, with real discernment, are conscious of a harsh note that is clearly not of God. Such an experience may easily take place when a believer is in the midst of spiritual warfare, when he is interacting with others, or even when he is preaching or teaching, if he is not careful. The energizing power that seeks to influence him is demonic, and it tries either to directly influence his spirit or to affect him through his soulish emotions.

This influence on the human spirit by evil spirits, which counterfeit the work of God in a believer when he is no longer in harmony with the Holy Spirit, needs to be understood and detected by one who seeks to walk with God. He needs to know that because he is spiritual, his spirit is open to two forces of the spirit realm. If he thinks that only the Holy Spirit can influence him in the spiritual sphere, he is sure to be misled. If it were so, he would become infallible, but he needs to *"watch and pray"* (Matthew 26:41) and to seek to have *"the eyes of* [his] *understanding...enlightened; that* [he] *may know"* (Ephesians 1:18) the true workings of God.

The believer who is spiritual must ponder deeply the revelation of heavenly warfare that is given in the sixth chapter of Ephesians. He must also strive to know, to the fullest extent, what it really means to *"take...the whole armour of God,"* which he is to use in *"the evil day"* (Ephesians 6:13) of specific onslaughts by the Enemy.

The deep desire of the Spirit of God at the present time is the perfecting, or full ripening into maturity, of the members of the body of Christ, so that His appearing may quickly take place and the millennial reign of Christ and His coheirs be ushered in. This will bring peace to the world. It will also bring about the defeat of Satan, who will then be cast down into the pit, when the kingdoms of the world will become *"the kingdoms of our Lord, and of his Christ"* (Revelation 11:15).

> *"Amen. Even so, come, Lord Jesus."*
> *—Revelation 22:20*